T0380181

ADAM & STEVE:
MIND, BODY & SOUL
WORKBOOK
DR. DEBBIE WILLIAMS

Copyright © 2022 by Dr. Debbie Williams. 827948

All rights reserved. No part of this book may be reproduced
or transmitted in any form or by any means, electronic or
mechanical, including photocopying, recording, or by any
information storage and retrieval system, without permission
in writing from the copyright owner.

Scripture quotations marked KJV are from the Holy Bible,
King James Version (Authorized Version). First published
in 1611. Quoted from the KJV Classic Reference Bible,
Copyright © 1983 by The Zondervan Corporation.

To order additional copies of this book, contact:
Xlibris
844-714-8691
www.Xlibris.com
Orders@Xlibris.com

ISBN: 978-1-6698-2659-0 (sc)
ISBN: 978-1-6698-2660-6 (hc)
ISBN: 978-1-6698-2658-3 (e)

Print information available on the last page

Rev. date: 06/09/2022

My Beliefs

I am of the Apostolic Faith, I believe the Bible is the inspired word of God written by the Holy Men of God, I believe in the death, burial and resurrection of my LORD and Savior Jesus Christ. I believe in One Lord, One Faith, One Baptism (Ephesians 4:5). Immersion in water for the remission of sins, and the indwelling of the Holy Ghost with the evidence of speaking in tongues as the spirit of God gives utterance. (The doctrine Jesus taught the disciples).

I am a "Holy Roller", I am not ashamed. I believe in living a Holy sanctified life, God has showed up in my life, and done an awesome thing, in me he has renewed me and made me whole in him and I have to thank and praise him. Period

Words to live by:

A-lways

P-raying

O-vercoming

S-in

T-rusting

O-ur

L-ord

I-n

C-hrist Jesus

"The law of the LORD is perfect, converting the soul; the testimony of
the Lord is sure, making wise the simple." PSALM 19:7

"Saving Souls from Strongholds"

I'm Dr. Debbie Williams, Thank you for taking the time to learn about "Strongholds" and breaking the cycle of sin in your life. I am happy to share this information with you, as well as my personal story of breaking free from the Strongholds that had me bond. Yes strongholds with am "S" because it was more than one. God is saving souls from strongholds, today even now.

This Workbook can be used as a companion book to my book, "Adam and Steve, My flesh; my desire, a book in which I tell my story of how God delivered me. This Workbook, "Adam & Steve: Mind, Body & Soul" is designed to help those who maybe struggling with Sexual Sin including, "Homosexuality", this workbook can help. You will learn Steps you can use to either help yourself or someone you know and love who is struggling with any Sexual Sin.

Because we live in a world where our fleshly desires can and do drive us, it is important to be knowledgeable of today's culture of "I," (self) and the "Me Spirit". This is what "I" want to, "I" feel like doing this, this feel's good to "me" so why not do it, I'm not hurting anyone it's a generation about "Me, Myself and I", and it's Satan's way of thinking. He wanted to be in charge, he wanted to be GOD.

Homosexuality has its roots buried in these types of sayings... "This is how "I" feel inside", this is the real "me"… <u>That's a lie from the pit.</u> All Satan needs is a foot hole.

As you read further you will be able to see your desires clearly and what's driving them. The question is Are your desires driven by God or Satan/flesh? We have all been driven by the "I" Spirit (self/flesh) at one time or another. My goal as a minister is to help you recognize it, discontinue it and live a life for GOD!

The Principles are simple to follow, Address the Mind, Body & Soul, The idea in renewing your Mind, Body & Soul with the Holy Ghost as your guide, by taking a real conscience look at your life and what we are allowing our minds and, bodies to do. By focusing on Christ, our Mind, Body and Soul will follow.

Sincerely,

Dr. Debbie Williams

Table of Contents

ADAM & STEVE:

MIND, BODY & SOUL WORKBOOK

INTRODUCTORY, ISSUES

Sexual Sin, is the one of the most prevalent sins we face today, this type of sin is a "Stronghold". This stronghold is hard to overcome. Especially on your own, but with the help of the Holy Spirit and a made up Mind, you can be free. Temptations will still come your way, James 1:14. But you will be able to face them, and not falter with the Holy Spirit living inside of you. Don't give into sin, any longer sexual sin or otherwise. James 1: 12.

Whatever your Mind buys into your Body will follow. It all starts in your Mind. As a thought, then you "foster it" (let it grow) then it becomes an action or deed James 1:15. This Workbook will teach you to STOP at the very thought of sin. You don't have to take sin to the next level, which is commenting the act (Sin). NIV 2 Corinthians 10:5, "We demolish arguments and every pretention that sets itself up against the knowledge of God. We take captive every thought, to make it obedient to Christ." This Workbook not only focuses on Homosexuality, but other sexual sins, including Fornication, Pedophilia (M.A.P) Minor Attracted Persons, Incest, Beastiality just to name a few.

Working with people to help conquer their sexual sins, with the Word of God, as my guide, and the Holy Ghost, to reveal the truth about the sexual immorality that we face today. You can truly be made whole if you so desire, with the Lord Jesus Christ.

These types of "Spirits" become attached to you and they influence you to commit these and other acts, Luke 22:3. This can bring pleasure to your flesh, or even monetary gain in some cases. You are still accountable for the acts done in your body! You have free will!

These "Strongholds" are hard to break, even when you know its wrong it can be hard to stop doing things that bring physical pleasure, even if you know it can cause you pain in the end. Some feel like it's just too hard to even try and fight, this type of thinking will have you given up before you even start. Now more than ever we have become a "right now" generation of people, we don't think about tomorrow when we commit a sin, in the sense of where we will spend eternity. I'm telling you it's not worth your Soul, nothing is.

My desire is to help those who want to help themselves, but just don't know how. Those who are torn and want to know the facts about sexual sins. This Workbook addresses your Mind, Body & Soul, each must be involved and addressed. To be "Holy" means to be set apart. We have limits and borders we can't cross, we, those that are Christian are a called out people and must live as such.

"For the grace of God that bringeth salvation hath appeared to all men, Teaching us that denying ungodliness and worldly lust, we should live soberly, righteously, and godly in this present world; Looking for that blessed hope, and the glorious appearing of the great God and our Savior Jesus Christ; Who gave himself for us, that he might redeem us from all iniquity, and purify unto himself a peculiar people, zealous of good works. These things speak and exhort, and rebuke, with all authority. Let no man despise thee". Titus 2: 11-15

This is why I wrote this book, we (the ones that know) are to Teach others God's word as he instructed us to do in, 2 Timothy Chapter 4: 2-5. It's up to you to chose to obey his word and not cave into any desires you my have that are not pleasing to God. This Workbook has very little of my opinion, I focus on what the Word of God says. Use the King James Version of the bible. All the scriptures are right here in one place. This book can help you work through any issues you may have or it can used as information to help someone else who is struggling. Either way this workbook is a must have for any Pastor, Youth Pastor, or Ministry leader.

This is your Workbook, feel free to notate, and highlight as you see fit, let's get started.

DEFINITIONS TO KNOW

Homosexuality- a romantic attraction, sexual behavior between members of the same sex or gender.

Heterosexual- people who are attracted, sexually or romantically to members of the opposite sex.

S.S.A. - Same Sex Attraction

Sin- An offence against God, an immoral act, transgression against God's law James 4:17

Immoral sex – Fornication, whoredom or unchastity connected with prostitution and or worship of fertility gods.

Transgender- personal identity and or gender that does not correspond with their birth sex.

Hermaphrodite- intersex someone born with ambiguous genitalia that is indiscernibly male or female.

Gender Fluid – non-conforming into binary gender categories, "man" or "woman"

Non- binary – this group of people may identify as having two or more genders (being bi- gender or tri -gender) or having no gender (genderless)

Gender Spectrum- to convey a wider range of gender identity and or expression than typically associated with the binary gender system.

Demi- gender- is a gender identity of a person identifying partially or mostly with one gender and at the same time with another gender.

Gender Neutral Pronouns- They, their, them

Gender Specific pronouns- her, or him Mx. Instead of Ms., Miss or Mr.

Pan- Sexual- being attracted to all gender identities, or attracted to people regardless of gender.

Pedophilia- an intense, recurrent sexual urges towards prepubescent children.

Prepubescent- the period preceding to puberty.

Chemical Imbalance- theory that is often cited as an explanation for some mental disorders.

Incest- human sexual activity between family members, close relatives.

M.A.P.- Minor Attracted Persons

Reprobate Mind -a sinful mind when a person doesn't care about the things of God 2 Tim 3:8

Attraction- the action or power of evoking interest in or liking for someone or some thing

Divers Lust- emphasize multiplicity, different, many.

Lust- Strong desire, longing to be, consumed with.

Bestiality- sexual intercourse involving a human and an animal.

Effeminate- having characteristics regarded as typical of a woman, unmanly 1 Cor 6:9

Fasting & Prayer- to go for a set time without food, water, sex, No unnecessary conversation, spending time in prayer to God for a specific need.

Untoward Generation- difficult to guide, manage, unruly.

Temptation- strong desire to do something wrong or unwise, urge itch- impulse, inclination.

Pagan Worship- A worship of multiple deities/ gods.

S & M – A term that stands for Sadism and Masochism, (Sadomasochism) often stereotyped as nonconsensual. A sexual orientation or behavior

Sadism- A wants complete control and compliance he wants his victim to feel fear. It is this fear that turns him on sexual sadists tend to relate to people in terms of power.

B and D- bondage and discipline, practices involving physical restraint and punishment.

These are just a few of the definitions you will need to know.

Look up any more definitions you want to know and list them here.

FROM THE AUTHORS HEART

I was lead by God to write Adam & Steve, My Flesh My desire I fought against telling story for many years, who wants to bear their soul for the world to see? Not many hands go up for that one. God laid on my heart, "how are you going to help anybody sitting on your testimony"? My reply was "lord I don't want anyone to know the things I've done, I don't want anyone to "judge me", after all I was in good standing <u>now</u> at my church and didn't want to take a chance of anyone shining me, after all the heart of man will turn on you in an instant.

But I was just thinking about myself and how I felt, I didn't give much thought about the people that I could help with my testimony. Living in sin lead me down the wrong path. Which put me in situations that caused me physical harm, from date rape, drinking and driving, domestic violence, sleeping around, partly trying to prove to myself I wasn't bi/gay. Going back in forth between men and women. I even had thoughts of suicide, wanting to take my own life.

After all that, I finally heeded the voice of the Lord, God you have me. You never know who you can help, even if it's just one person it's worth it, to share your story.

"Dearly beloved, I beseech you as strangers and pilgrims, abstain from fleshly lust, which war against the soul;" 1 Peter 2:11

"And likewise also the men, leaving the natural use of the woman, burned in their lust one toward another; men with men working that which is unseemly, and receiving in themselves that recompense of their error which was meet. And even as they did not like to retain God in their knowledge, God gave them over to a reprobate Mind, to do those things which are not convenient;" Romans 1:27- 28

"For if we sin willfully after we have received the knowledge of the truth, there remaineth no more sacrifice for sins," Hebrews 10:26

Jesus was slain, so that you would be free, he died on the cross to set you free, the bondage of sin, and the penalty of death. Don't volunteer to be a slave to sin, once you have been freed from it the price was paid in full.

Jesus backed, the creation story, affirming the biblical version of marriage in Matthew 19.

SECTION 1: ADDRESSING THE MIND, BODY AND SOUL

Before we start, fill in the chart below that way we can track your progress at the end of this Workbook.

How do you feel about your lifestyle today? Are you happy with it?	Why are you reading this Workbook? Knowledge, For yourself or someone else?	What do you expect to gain by reading / working in this book?
Once you can see it,	You can identify it	Then address it
What are 2 of your best Qualities? 1. 2.	What can you bring to the body of Christ?	Describe 3 of your characteristics? 1. 2. 3.

What is your favorite scripture year to date write it out here?

_____

_____

_____

Have you read this scripture in the various version? Write it in a different version here.

_____

_____

_____

What makes this your favorite Scripture, describe it in your own words

_____

_____

_____

What would you like to receive from this work book (example personal growth, spiritual peace, healthier relationships)?

_____

_____

_____

When will you know you have reached your goals (explain what that will look like)?

_____

_____

_____

What barriers do you expect to face while renewing your walk with Christ?

_____

_____

_____

Who can support you on your journey to freedom from bondage? It's important to know who you maybe can count on before trouble comes.

_____

_____

When you are able to put a finger on an issue your facing that's standing in your way, between "self / flesh" and a oneness with God you will be better equip address those issues, and to stop them.

REAL Christians love others … and help where ever they can to encourage those who maybe struggling with Sin. REAL Christians don't bash

What am I really fighting against?

We are going to take a real look at the truth no matter where it leads us. (This was my thought when I started my journey and sought the LORD for the truth for myself when I was in sin.) I had a willingness to honestly know the truth no matter what I'd fine.

The Mind, Body and Soul are all connected. To get optimal results you will need to address each of the three areas. Good Mental, Physical, Spiritual health are equally important to the over all man/ woman. There are no quick fixes here, this will take you some time to master. Change can be difficult your body is used to certain stimuli and will crave it. Your body wants to keep doing the same old thing it has been doing YOU will have to put your body under subjection on a regular basis.

Each person's journey is different, take your time, don't stress out over hurdles or set backs, PRAY and read your BIBLE and pick yourself up and start again, I too had a few slip ups, along the way, but God is faithful. Jesus is KEY.

If we are truly concerned about building up parts of our mental, physical spiritual health, then a turning away from sin is in order, we then need to prayerfully review what we will have to change in our lives. Take time today to pray and ask God what his plan is for your life.

In order to fight effectively, you have to know what you're fighting against. Satan disguises himself as "an angel of light." "For such are false apostles deceitful workers, transforming themselves into the apostles of Christ. And no marvel; for Satan himself is transformed into an angel of light. Therefore it is no great thing if his ministers also be transformed as the ministers of righteousness; whose end shall be according to their works." 2 Corinthians 11: 13-15 Satan can appear as a angel he is not who he appears to be and neither are his minister's / the false prophets. (A false prophet is a person who falsely claims to be sent by God, and or doesn't teach the word of God.)

The bible is your weapon, against sin, you must know it to use it. It has the scriptures you need. You must rely on God's word, and his spirit to get you through every day, you cannot do it on your own. Praying to God for healing, Read the bible daily, learn it, by knowing a few scriptures by heart and being able to recall it in times of troubles / temptations can help and uplift you. "For though we walk in the flesh, we do not war after the flesh: (For the weapons of our warfare are not carnal, but mighty through God to the pulling down of strong holds;) 2 Corinthians 10 : 3-4

You can't fight your flesh's desires on your own you need God's Holy Spirit to be successful, and this is NOT a one time thing, you must rely on Jesus every single day, every minute. This battle is an everyday, every minute kind of fight. We must stay vigilant and guard ourselves daily from everything that can/

will lead us back into sin sexual or other wise. This may include limiting and or cutting out some family members, friends, T.V. shows even some music. All these things can lead you back into a life of sin and keep you in a sinful life if your not careful. Been there too. People can and will influence you to stay in a life of sin for whatever reason.

Satan deceives people and makes sin look good, appealing, and even normal, he makes doing well and right, look boring and wrong. Genesis 3:1-3 "Now the serpent was more subtil than any beast of the field which the LORD God had made. And he said unto the woman, Yea, hath God said, Ye shall not eat of every tree of the garden? And the women said unto the serpent, we may eat of the fruit of the trees of the garden: But of the fruit of the tree which is in the midst of the garden, God hath said, Ye shall not eat of it, neither shall ye touch it, lest ye die."

Satan in the "form" of the serpent said "Yea hath God said, Ye shall not eat of every tree of the garden? Eve told the serpent what Adam had told her (verse 3) and the serpent said "Ye shall not surely die". He said "God knows the day you eat of this tree your eyes shall be opened and you shall be as gods, knowing good and evil".

By knowing where Eve went wrong we can avoid that trap in our own lives. "But I fear, lest somehow, as the serpent deceived Eve by his craftiness, so your Minds may be corrupted from the simplicity that is in Christ". 2 Corinthians 11:3 Satan left out the part about sin causing separation for God, and how a spiritual death incurs. Satan tempted Eve with his sly and cunning ways and choice of words, as he still does today to us. Once we begin to see that giving into temptations or a temporary pleasure, (an external pleasure to the body) comes with deadly results, those that are strong in the Lord must cry out aloud against sin as stated in Isaiah 58:1.

Why is it important to know how Satan operates?

_____

_____

_____

Anytime a man is controlled by the wants of his flesh, thoughts he is out of control! Think on What or who motivates you to commit these actions? Think about how these types of desires start.

Would you agree they start in your Mind as an idea or thought? Maybe even something you've seen?

What is your Top Priority? If it's not God then you have a problem, God comes first in your life.

Whatever you are controlled / ruled by.. (ie ..Money, sex, power) has the "POWER" over you, and you're a slave to it.

Write out below, 2 Peter 2:19 King James Version (kjv)

_____

_____

_____

_____

_____

What did Jesus say in John 8:34? Why is that important?

_____

_____

_____

    Addictions will cause you to lose control, and if you're not in control than the addiction is, (Satan) it's what drives you (and reason goes out the window). Giving into Addictions i.e... Your flesh causes separation from God. Read Romans 8:8 Admit you have an addiction, Read Proverbs 28:13 Ask God in Prayer to deliver you from sin, Read Matt 18:18 and resist the devil James 4:7-8

    How will you address these areas? Write your plan, include Pray and scripture reading time, set your goals and put them into action. Include all three areas Mind, Body and Soul, Be honest with yourself.

Identify anything that might be standing in the way of you meeting your goals? Is there an addiction you're missing? Does the T.V. shows you watch that encourage homosexual behavior or Sexual Immorality? Do your family or friends encourage you to be "Yourself" and tell you just to live your life?

You don't want to be yourself, in us, that is to say our flesh dwells no good thing. Your desire should be what God is calling for you to be. Your fleshly desires are not of God. Your desire should be to be a new creature in HIM / Christ. Why would anyone want to be themselves? Sexual Immorality leads to other Sins... Sexual and other wise, and it will never be enough your body/flesh will want more and more. These are just a <u>few</u> places sexual sin will take you.

Pornography	Bestiality	Drugs & Alcoholic
Homosexuality	Menage a trois	Pedophilia
Masturbation	S & M	Rape
Rough Sex	Bondage	

Remember this Workbook is yours to work in, List a few things you need to work on, whether listed or not.

_____

_____

_____

_____

With God we can accomplish anything. God isn't calling us to be ourselves, He is calling us to be a new creatures in HIM, and old things must pass away. The old things you once did you can no longer, do.

An Addiction doesn't always mean drugs or alcohol, you can be addicted to porn, sex, food, gossip etc.

It's time to Meditate

Read these scriptures below think on them, Write what they are saying to you.

"Let this Mind be in you, which was also in Christ Jesus," Philippians 2:5

_____

_____

_____

"I beseech you therefore, brethren, by the mercies of God, that ye present your bodies a living sacrifice, holy, acceptable unto God, which is your reasonable service." Romans 12:1 Describe How you can present your body as a living sacrifice?

_____

_____

_____

"For what is man profited, if he shall gain the whole world, and lose his soul? Or what shall a man give in exchange for his soul?" Matt 16:26

_____

_____

_____

"Cry aloud, spare not, life up thy voice like a trumpet, and shew my people their transgression" "For we wrestle not against flesh and blood, but against principalities, against powers, against the rulers of darkness of this world, against spiritual wickedness in high places". Ephesians 6:12

We must take the time to seek God now while he can be found.

Do you want to be free from Sexual Sin? _____

Why do you want to be free from Sexual Sin? Has Sexual immorality affected your life in a negative way? Are you ready and willing to make a change today? _____

On the surface these seems like an easy questions, but they require some honest thought. This is something that you have to do for yourself in order for it to work. Walking away from sin is not easy but it can be done. But know Satan doesn't want to let you go, he will work extra hard to keep you locked in a sinful lifestyle. Are you ready and willing to change your life? It will require some work on your part.

Scripture Reading:

John 14: 14 "If ye shall ask anything in my name, I will do it."

You must ask in Jesus' name, Pray and ask the Lord to teach you how to live for him, Read the holy bible find a few uplifting gospel songs to play and sing. Surround yourself with the people of God join a ministry in a church trust the Lord and read his word daily. You can't always carry a bible with you make yourself some flash cards of helpful scriptures to read.

Read the Lord's Prayer (this a great scripture to learn, by heart and repeat to yourself in times of trouble)

Our Father which art in heaven,

Hallowed be thy name.

Thy Kingdom come.

Thy will be done in earth,

as it is in heaven.

Give us this day our daily bread.

And forgive us our debts,

as we forgive our debtors.

And lead us not into temptation,

but deliver us from evil:

For thine is the kingdom,

and the power,

and glory forever.

Amen

_____

_____

_____

_____

_____

_____

_____

_____

_____

_____

_____

Matthew 6: 9-13 (The Lords Prayer)

What is the Lord's Prayer saying over all to you?

_____

_____

_____

Don't be discouraged if you don't feel the Lord answering right away, continue to seek him. By meditating on the Lord and his word daily you will leave no room for Satan to enter in. By keeping busy kingdom building you will put God's business above your own thoughts and ideas thus putting Satan's will under your feet.

By focusing on the Lord you will have less time think on sinful things. (The Living Bible) Proverbs 16:27-29 "Idle hands are the devil's workshop; idle lips are his mouthpiece. An evil man sows strife; gossip separates the best of friends. Wickedness loves company and leads others into sin.

Idle hands can lead to sin, a idle person is likely to comment sin. It is important to stay busy inside the house of the Lord to be accountable to the building of the kingdom of God. Give you talents and time to the cause of Jesus Christ. It's not enough to just attend a service, devote the time and energy you gave, when you where living in sin even more so.

"Hear counsel, and receive instruction, that thou mayest be wise in thy latter end." Proverbs 19:20

Create a gospel playlist, Here some of mine:

He's Alright … Edwin Hawkins

Worthy Vessel ……Carole Allen Simmons

Never Would've Made it …..Marvin Sapp

Mary did you Know…. CeeLo Green

He's My Rock…. Bri Babineaux

Rise Again…. Dallas Holms

Something about the Name Jesus …Kirk Franklin

What's your gospel song go to playlist In times of trouble? If you don't have a playlist get one.

1. _____

2. _____

3. _____

4. _____

STEP 1: MIND, BODY & SOUL, AND BY CLEANING OUT YOUR MENTAL CLOSET

Getting your mind right! With The Holy Spirit, Prayer & Fasting, along with Reading the bible is All Key to Your Success. Your fleshly desires won't rule you, any longer you will rule over it, your body is subject to the Holy Spirit in you. You need the Holy Ghost!

Paul said in 1 Corinthians 9: 27 "But I keep under my body, and bring it into subjection: lest that by any means, when I have preached to others, I myself should be a castaway."

Biblical teaching in this area is straight forward, surprisingly some Christians allow the world to take the affections and compromise their values. Too many church leaders have forsaken the wonderful task of making the Word of God known in the World today, thank God for those Christian leaders who faithfully Teach, Preach and live Holy Lives.

Cleaning out your Mental Closet is not enough you have to clean out your Natural Physical closet too. Cross dressers and or Trans Gender People must become new also by letting the "old Man" die completely through baptism, in water in Jesus's Name.

"The woman shall not wear which pertaineth unto a man, neither shall a man put on a woman's garment: for all that do so are abomination unto the LORD thy God."

Notice the Word "Garment" is used here not Pants or even Skirts, whatever "Garment Pertains" to a woman, God left no loop hole here!

It's ALL about your INTENT.. The Why your doing it. Is your desire to look/feel more like a man or a woman when you wear those garments?

You must have the Holy Ghost (Spirit) to fight your fleshly desires and Win!!

You cannot do it on your OWN.

Romans 13:14 "But put ye on the Lord Jesus Christ, and make not provision for the flesh, to fulfill the lusts thereof."

John 14:15- 16 "If ye love me, keep my commandments. (16) And I will pray the Father, and he shall give you another comforter, that he may abide with you forever;" (that comforter is the Holy Ghost).

Ephesians 5:17- 18 "Wherefore be ye not unwise, but understanding what the will of the Lord is. And be not drunk with wine, wherein is excess; but be filled with the Spirit;"

You can't fight any Stronghold without the Holy Ghost, Prayer and Fasting!!

There are several "Strongholds", A Sexual Strongholds, is one of the strongest strongholds there are. I want to talk about the "spirit of Homosexuality". Since hardly no one wants to really talk about it, along with other Sexual sins, these are done in the flesh (our bodies). Remember, our bodies are from God, we chose what they can and can not do.

Scripture Reading:

1 Corinthians 6:15- "Know ye not that your bodies are the members of Christ? Shall I then take the members of Christ, and make them the members of a harlot? God forbid. What? Know ye not that he which is joined to a harlot is one body? For two, saith he, shall be one flesh. But he that is joined unto the Lord is one spirit. Flee fornication. Every sin that a man doeth is without the body; but he that committeth fornication sinneth against his own body. What? Know ye not that your body is the temple of the Holy Ghost which is in you, which ye have of God, and ye are not your own?"

"God's judgment on homosexuality/ lesbian relationships is not because God is a "killjoy", but because he is opposed to what kills joy." John Piper

Which Scripture will you refer to, that you have read thus far to help you on your Journey? And why did you pick that scripture?

_____

_____

_____

In order to be helped you have to admit you have a problem…

1 John 1:9 "If we confess our sins, he is faithful and just to forgive us our sins, and to cleanse us from all unrighteousness."

The first step in getting on the right track is admitting you have a problem. This can be hard to do No one wants to admit they have a sexual related problem. They may feel embarrassment, fear and or shame. But it is a step toward healing. Look we all have some sort of desires. Any act or desire not of God must be discontinued it's not worth your soul!

If I can admit to myself that I have a problem I can work at finding the solution to my problem.

"Then Peter said unto them, Repent, and be baptized every one of you in the name of Jesus Christ for the remission of sins, and ye shall receive the gift of the Holy Ghost." Acts 2:38

Acknowledge your doubts, Fears, then you can address them, Is there anything stopping you from moving forward right now?

_____

_____

_____

_____

_____

_____

_____

What Road Blocks are you facing today that hinder your relationship with God? You can only address your issues if you know what they are.

Be honest with yourself. I'm never going to see your answers anyway.

_____

_____

_____

What do you like most about yourself?

_____

_____

_____

Are you Afraid that will change?

_____

_____

_____

Read Matt 6:9-13 Write the scripture out below

_____

_____

_____

This is a "activity" about my friend "John who feels like he might be gay, he doesn't know what to do, and he is afraid to tell his family. He wants to serve God what would you say to him? Sometimes we can give advice to others better than we can take it.

_____

_____

_____

_____

_____

Do you depend on others to validate you?

_____

_____

<u>Notes or any question.</u>

Closing Section Prayer: Dear Lord, forgive me of my sins, that I have done unto you and thank you, God for letting me see the era of my ways, I will pray and listen to your direction that you have set before me, help me to finished the good work you have started in my life, I know I can do all things, through Christ who strengthens me, Amen

STEP 2: SETTING YOUR MIND, BODY AND SOUL FREE FROM "STRONGHOLDS"

1 Thessalonians 5:23 "And the very God of peace sanctify you wholly; and I pray God your whole Spirit and Soul and Body be preserved blameless unto the coming of our Lord Jesus Christ."

Mind	Body	Soul
Are you Ready and willing to change? You must take this step for yourself! (John 14:15)	Change your style of dress, Change your attitude, anything that identifies with living a sinful lifestyle..(tight or revealing cloths) You are a new creature look like it. Joshua 24:1)	Repent for your sins against God. Have you been Baptized In the name of the Lord Jesus Christ? If not do so as per Acts 2:38, Ephesians 1:7
You must stay dedicated to the change process. Nothing happens overnight, give yourself a chance to truly make a change. Isaiah 26:3-5	Your body is a temple and you can not let any and everything enter into it, Sex, drugs and alcohol. (Beware of replacing one addiction for another.) 1 Peter 5:8	Forgive yourself, this can be hard to do once you realize the gravity of your sins. Matthew 6:14
Purpose in your mind to change. Be aware of your thoughts, your old memories will creep back in rebuke it in the name of Jesus, and pray. 2 Corinthians 5:17	Stay in the house of the Lord as much as possible. Join a ministry you want to limit your free time as much as possible. Psalms 37:4	Give yourself over to the will of God. Romans 12:1-2

Romans 12:2 1	Corinthians 6:9- 11, 13	Jude 1:5-7

Circle the scripture that helped you the most and write it out. By reading and writing it out you will have a better chance of remembering it it times of need.

_____

_____

_____

Now write what that scripture means to you.

_____

_____

_____

How can you Address Your Mind, Body and Soul using this grid? What changes in your life can you make today? What changes can you make over time? Add it to the grid.

Mind	Body	Soul
Today 1. 2.	Today 1. 2.	Today 1. 2.
Future Goals	Future Goals	Future Goals
What scripture can help in this area?	What scripture can help in this area?	What scripture can help in this area?

Set some realistic Goals in each of these areas, revisit your goals, to see how many you were able to keep. Jot down the one's that you had a hard time with and add them to you next future goal sheet.

Read each Scripture in the grid, again they will help you in your walk with Christ. Follow each step in the Mind, Body, & Soul grid, and clean out your mental closet. When your mind is stayed on God you have a better chance of rebuking ungodly thoughts. Don't give up you can do it!

"There hath no temptation taken you but such as is common to man: but God is faithful, who will not suffer you to be tempted above that ye are able; but will with the temptation also make a way to escape, that ye may be able to bear it." 1 Corinthians 10:13

What do you think will be the hardest thing to walk away from?

_____

_____

_____

"For ye are bought with a price: therefore glorify God in your body, and in your spirit, which are God's." 1 Corinthians 6: 20

Test your knowledge

What Does Satan Have to gain, by a person living a lifestyle caving into their flesh and it's desires?

_____

_____

_____

Draw a line and Match the Scripture with the correct step on the grid of Mind, Body, & Soul:

Mind- In whom we have redemption through his blood, the forgiveness of sins,

    According to the riches of his grace.

Body- If ye love me, keep my commandments.

Soul- Delight thyself also in the LORD; and he shall give thee the desires of thine heart.

Draw a line and Match the word to it's definition. When you have a clear understanding of words and their meanings you can make a more informed decisions.

1. Fornication: A. Exceptionally
                            Loathsome
                            Hateful sinful
                            Wicked

2. Stronghold:

    B. Romantic
    Attraction
    Sexual behavior
    Between same
    Sex gender.

3. Homosexuality:

    C. Ongoing
    Struggle of
    Habits
    Emotions
    Thoughts in
    Our mind we're
    Unable to break

4. .Abomination:

    D. Having or
    Showing hate or
    Dislike

5. Homophobic:

    E. Sexual intercourse between
    Unmarried people.

6. Adultery:

    F. Strong sexual desire
    Crave

7. Holy-

    G. Voluntary sexual intercourse with
    A person who is
    Not your spouse.

8. Lust:

    H. Set a part
    Called out

Activity: I need your help, My friend "John" is having a hard time letting go of his pass desires, what would you say to encourage him?

_____

_____

_____

_____

_____

Your attitude affects your decisions, and you need to know the difference between what you want and what you actually need. Ask God to open your eyes to what you really need verses what your flesh desires.

As a result of keeping God's commandments, your life will be better in the following areas?

_____

_____

_____

Write out Philippians 4:19

_____

_____

_____

Why is this scripture important?

_____

_____

_____

Closing Section Prayer:

Dear Lord, in your word you have challenged me to be Aware and prepared, Lord hold me and keep me let your spirit guide me to accept the changes I need to make in my life, Amen.

Notes

SECTION 2: WAS I BORN GAY?

This has been the basis for a lot of discussion over the years. I was one of those people who said, "I was born Gay", Bi- sexual to be more specific. Feeling as it was part of me like my hands and feet are. I was on the "You are born Gay Band Wagon," after all I could remember being attracted to women as well as men (boys), since I was a child (I talk more about this in my book, "Adam and Steve, My Flesh, my Desire). Later In life I Identified as Bi-sexual, because I felt it suited my desires me better.

I couldn't understand it. Why do people feel any way that is contrary to the word of God? This question just kept ringing in my mind. I started to look at the bigger picture after a conversation with my mom. Who or what has something to gain out of all of this? By believing I was born Gay I was more incline to be "myself" sort of speak because this is who I am inside, right? Even if God's word was contrary to it.

What about those who say we should be able to for fill our desires as long as we are not hurting anyone. But what about the men who have a desire to rape? Or the men who desire young boys to have sex with? Of course you would say no, not them. You can't pick and choose which sin is "OK" because none of them are ok, Or safer, or less violent.

I looked deeper and asked myself more questions, no matter what I'd find, I wanted answers. What if it was Satan and he was actually doing like the church was saying he was doing? (Any good researcher must explore all avenues) Satan knew man was precious in the sight of God, he already persuaded a 3rd of the angles to follow him. How hard would it be to persuade man (Man- Kind) into believing he was gay and even born gay? I was reminded what happened with Eve in the garden, in the book of Genesis. So I went on a journey of reading my bible to find out. Anything I could find on Spirits, Satan, God's love for man because it all played a part In if Satan's really behind this feeling I have or not.

This research took a lot of reading and a lot of time. I asked myself would Satan really go to all that trouble? Is Satan really that cunning? Reading about the spirits that were in the people through out the bible, and how spirits really had people doing all kinds of things, including hurting themselves. Was it possible? And the answer was Yes it is possible.

But I needed more than a yes it's possible. This was how I felt and I wanted to know why. Is this how I was born? Or is there something else going on here I found Romans 7:8, "For I know that in me (that is, in my flesh,) dwelleth no good thing: for to will is present with me; but how to perform that which is good I find not."

James 1:2-4, "My brethren, count it all joy when you fall into divers temptations knowing this, that the trying of your faith works patience. But let patience have her perfect work, that you may be perfect and entire wanting nothing."

- "And the Lord said, who shall persuade Ahab, that he may go up and fall at Ramoth-gilead? And one said on this manner, and another said on that manner. <u>And there came forth a spirit, and stood before the LORD, and said I will persuade him.</u> And the LORD said unto him, Wherewith? And he said, I Will go forth, and I will be a lying Spirit in the mouth of all the prophets. And he said, Thou shalt persuade him, and prevail also: go forth, and do so." 1 Kings 22: 20-22

Through the allurement of sin, comes your testing. The goal is to come through your test or temptations victorious.

James 1:13-14 " Let no man say when he is tempted, I am tempted of God for God can not be tempted with evil, neither tempts he any man. But every man is tempted, when he drawn away of his own lust, and enticed."

We just read a spirit went out and persuaded… Ahab's prophets (Read the chapter) which were false prophets, they were already lairs and unjust mean, that how the spirit was able to enter them. What does that tell you? Did anyone influence your lifestyle?

_____

_____

_____

If your mind is stayed on God and your busy kingdom building you can't fall prey to Satan's devices .. (I'm Not saying you won't go through anything. look at Job) why? Because as soon as God's people get the thought to waver or sin they will <u>immediately</u> put these thoughts out of there minds and call on the blood of Jesus.. it sounds so simple right? With God all things are possible.

Who tempted Jesus in Matt chapter 4? What did Jesus say each time he was tempted.

_____

_____

1.

2.

3.

Why did that work?

_____

_____

_____

What Did Michael say, in Jude 1:9

_____

_____

If I told you fleshly desires was your test, of obedience your trail to overcome before you could make it to heaven, would that change your mindset?

Well it is, Every one has something to over come.

Why does God allow these test and trails?

Test and trails are the only way we know for sure, what areas of our lives we are spiritually strong in and what areas we are spiritually weak in. Once you can recognize this you can grow in the areas you are weaker in, and even help others. Test and trails build up your faith every time you pass a test your faith grows.

We say we love Jesus no matter what, well it's time to prove it.

We say we will be faithful, but how do we know for sure unless we're tested in the areas we long for or desire.

To know your area of weaknesses is the beginning of being free from it's hold.

I believe HOMOSEXUALITY is a type of learned behavior, whether consciously or subconsciously (the unconscious beliefs, ideas and reactions to life around us that literally drives our life without our knowledge.. on a subconscious level we maybe unaware) My own experiences and reading the bible for myself opened my eyes to the truth and it wasn't pretty.

Think on the styles of cloths your kids like, if your kids are anything like mine they like the same kinds of styles that the other kids are wearing, they have learned from just watching the other kids in the community in which they live.

God created us, (man) he loves man (us) he took the time to make us this beautiful planet with everything we could need. He spent time with man in the garden of Eden. When you look at Genesis and recount the creation of everything that was made for man you see a loving God. When you read about Moses, giving the Children of Israel, God's instructions after coming down off the Mount, when you see all he has done over time, yet man still sinned (disobeyed) and still God loved us and took us back unto himself.

Example, we are not supposed to tell lies, did God make us lair? Just because we have the ability to lie. In reading the bible you see Satan came in and tricked Eve into disobeying God, so I had to ask myself could it be true? Could he trick me? No one wants to believe they are being coned or tricked, no one wants to believe that they are being used for someone's else's purpose. We all want to believe that we are doing what " we want to do," we're a strong minded people and we at least know our own bodies and desires. Right?

Roman 8:6-9 "For to be carnally minded is death; but to be spiritually minded is life and peace. Because the carnal mind is enmity against God: for it is not subject to the law of God, neither indeed can be. So then they that are in the flesh can not please God. But ye are not in the flesh, but in the Spirit, if so be that the spirit of God dwell in you. Now if any man have not the Spirit of Christ, he is none of his." Your not automatically able to just stand up against temptations you need the holy ghost to do so.

Read these scriptures in * Deut 18:9, Leviticus 18:22 -30 and Genesis 19: 1-12, .. pay close attention to verse number 4, "But before they lay down, the men of the city, even the men of Sodom, compassed the house round, both (old and young) all the people from every quarter."

Quote: "Concerning homosexuality: This once brought hell out of heaven on Sodom." Charles Spurgeon

How do we learn as people? We are taught, either by instruction or watching the behaviors and actions of others, for example I speak the English language because both my parents spoke English around me, when I was young, growing up I picked it up from them, now My grandmother spoke English and Spanish so in the summer time to get bye my sister and I picked up Spanish from her. She did not sit us down and teach us we heard her talking to other people and after a while we could speak a little Spanish.

In Genesis 19, The old men and the young me came and surrounded the house the young men had learned this behavior from the older men in their town no doubt, from just being with them and watching them (maybe even being victims of the men as well, however that is not mentioned here in scripture). Just spending time with a person can influence you to do the things they do. It can change how you do and see things as well.

T.V., radio and songs have been known to change the mood. You ever hear a song that just got you in the mood? Or watched a movie that made you cry? Saw A movie that scared you and you couldn't go to sleep? If you watch porn enough you'll eventually want to try what you see, you watch it enough you can become desensitized to it and/ or it can become a normal act to you. Guard your eye gate, be conscious to what you SEE and LISTEN to, Proverbs 4 20-22 turn your ear and eye gate to Jesus and his words and deeds, in the bible they are directly related to our physical bodies health, and our spiritual bodies health as well, we become stronger with his power and are able to wheel the sword of the word. If all we take into our spirit is the T.V., the cell phones calls we make, the comments of those who are not living right what do you think will come out of us? We can only think on or recall what is in us, if you haven't read any scriptures you won't be able to recall any in the time of need.

"Teaching us that, denying ungodliness and worldly lust, we should live soberly, righteously, and godly, in this present world;" Titus 2:12

"The heart is deceitful above all things, and desperately wicked: who can know it?" Jeremiah 17:9

Read Proverbs 22:6, " Train up a child in the way he should go: and when he is old, he will not depart from it.." Don't you know Satan knows the world of God? He quoted to Jesus in the book of Matt chapter 4.

Why do you think teaching our children is so important? How can we do a better job?

_____

_____

_____

What would you say to your child who told you they felt like they maybe gay?

_____

_____

_____

_____

_____

Titus chapter 2 talks about teaching.. the older women are to teach the younger women.. whether we know it or not our actions and lifestyle teacher's those around us who we are. You ever ask your child the question, "Why did you do that"? you get the answer "Well Sally did it," Kids copy what they see.

*Read Leviticus 18: 22-30

"Thou shalt not lie with mankind, as with womankind: it is Abomination

Neither shalt thou lie with any beast to defile thyself therewith: neither shall any woman stand before a beast to lie down thereto: it is confusion.

* Defile not yourselves in any of these things: for in all these the nations are defiled which I cast out before you: And the land is defiled: therefore I do visit the iniquity therefore upon it, and the land itself vomited out her inhabitants. Ye shall therefore keep my statues and my judgments, and shall not commit any of these abominations; neither any of your own nation, nor any stranger that sojourneth among you: (For all these abomination have the men of the land done. Which were before you, and the land is defiled;)"

• This is a warning not to do what the nations / people who were there before you had done.

Learned Behavior, don't pick their Habits, or their Traditions he's telling us not to do as they have done.. if you were born gay wouldn't Some of population of the children of Israel been living this way already? It wasn't a Stop doing, it was a don't start doing!!

"That the land spew not you out also, when ye defile it as it spewed out the nations that were before you. For whosoever shall commit any of these abominations, even the souls that commit them shall be cut off from among their people. Therefore shall ye keep mine ordinance, that ye commit not any one of these abominable customs, which were committed before you, and that ye defile not yourselves therein: I am the LORD your God."

Change takes some of us a little longer than others, that's ok. We must walk in the life of the Christian God is calling you to be. Don't become frustrated. Instead model the Christian life. Work on yourself, the way you dress, the way in which you think, the way you even speak, and have fun in God.

I find that those who are struggling with sexual identity issues, "Cross dressers or Transgender" May have a hard time finding who are or who they can be in Christ Joining the Men's ministry if your born a man is a great way for them to learn what it is to be a Christian male, it's the same with women, joining a Woman's Ministry can help you find and better the understand the Christian Woman who is inside of you.

What would you say now, to someone who tells you,"I can love and commit to whatever gender I please, it's my choice who I chose to marry"? Keep in mind we are not just trying to help ourselves but others if we can.

_____

_____

_____

_____

Why is it our Job as Christians to tell others the "Truth in Love"?

_____

_____

_____

What would you say to someone who was ashamed to seek Spiritual help from a pastor or minister?

_____

_____

_____

"John" wonders if being "born again "(of Water and Spirit) will really help him. What scriptures do you think will help him decide to be born again?

_____   _____   _____

"John" calls you and he tells you he still feels the same way after he is Baptized yesterday, What would you say to him?

_____

_____

_____

Learned Behavior

Let's talk about it, How can one learn to be Gay, Lesbian or Bi-sexual? I believe sexual spirits can enter in a persons body at any age there are a few avenues well talk about, but it all ends up being a spiritual influence at the end of it. By tracing a few stories to the very beginning I've learned that people are different and have very different stories, to tell. Some of these people suffered from repeated rape by the same sex perpetrator. Some by opposite sex perpetrators, or family members, there are rare cases the parent of a child want a girl, and got the opposite sex of what they wanted, leading to a child being trained on purpose and some inadvertently to act a certain way not in line with there birth sex. Watching porn with an parent or older sibling can normalize sex acts with genders of same sex, where it can start to appeal to you over time if the child is young enough. I mean the answers run from A-Z.

But they all were sexual sins in nature "like spirits" they run in the same spiritual circles. It's such a thin line between different sexual sins because many are into more than just one type of sexual sin.

One Lady I talked with said she had been done wrong by many different men that she wanted to be with a woman, she thought it would be better for her because women "understood" women better. She was already in many sexual relationships with men, which is also a sexual sin, and was now willing to try yet another sin. Trading one sin for another sin/ stronghold. Was this an excuse? Why was she so willing to pursue an homosexual way of life? It was admittedly unlike her. Could it be that with being "with so many men" as she put it, she had opened herself up to the "Spirit of Homosexuality". Now that made since to me If your involved in one sin that is close in nature to another sin you could be bound by many more sexual sins.

Matt 12: 45, " Then goeth he, and taketh with himself seven other spirits more wicked than himself, and they enter in and dwell there: and the last state of the man is worse than the first. Even so shall it be also unto this wicked generation."

But Honestly it makes very little difference how or why you became Gay. The spirit is the underline reason now. Homosexuality is a spirit a "stronghold" which influences in's host

Spirits can teach, the Holy spirit is a teacher, right? Likewise other spirits can teach or influence you as well.

*Read Deut 20:17-18 in the King James version "But thou shalt utterly destroy them; namely the Hittites, and the Amorites, the Canaanites, and the Perizzites, the Hivites and the Jebusites; as the LORD thy God hath commanded thee: (NEXT VERSE) That they teach you not to do after all their abominations, which they have done unto their gods; against the LORD your God.

The Holy Ghost can teach you how to dress how to live .. if you let it.. Exodus 31:3, " And I have filled him with the "Spirit of God" (Holy Ghost) in wisdom, and in understanding, and in knowledge, and in all manner of workmanship."

The Holy Spirit taught Bezaleel what and how to do the work of the LORD. The spirit had instructed him in what to do. The Holy Spirit can, and is willing to help us in every area of our lives if we let him. So what about an evil spirit?

Read Luke 22:3, "Then entered Satan into Judas surnamed Iscariot, being the number of the twelve." Judas was not an innocent by stander he allowed Satan to influence his decision, Judas had a choice, to betray Jesus or not to he let his greed take over, Luke 22:22"And truly the Son of man goeth, as it was determined: but woe unto that man by whom he is betrayed!"

What about "Legion?" in the book of Luke, this man had a home and had lived a normal life before the spirit entered him, he was pretty much naked and living in a tomb with the dead, cutting himself until he met Jesus and the spirits were cast out of him.

Spirits are Real.. where do you think they went after the pigs killed themselves?

You have a choice, By Saying you were Born this Way doesn't take your choice away!

.. "Have you not Read"?" that he which made them at the beginning made them male and female" according to Matt 19: 4. GOD ONLY CREATED 2 GENDERS Male and Female.

You must be Born again, No Matter how you feel you were Born, of the Water and of the Spirit to wash all your sins away.

Why do we have to be born again of the water and the spirit?

_____

_____

_____

*Because we are a called out people, can't live any kind of way! We must do our very best to be what God is Calling for. "There shall be no whore of the daughters of Israel, nor a Sodomite of the sons of Israel," Deut 23: 17

We're told to be Holy for he is Holy, to be set apart. We must have limits and borders we can't cross or we'd be just as the heathen. We must be transformed by God's word, conforming to the world nor allow it's standers to rule or govern our Christians Lives.

"Now the Spirit speaketh expressly, that in the latter times some shall depart from faith, giving heed to seducing spirits, and doctrines of devils; Speaking lies in hypocrisy; having their conscience seared with a hot iron;" 1 Tim 4:1-2

Paul is talking about a period of time, after the first coming of Christ and before his second coming, sounds like the times we are in were people will become in danger of Apostasy those not strong in the Lord or his Word will fall away or lose their way. We have some Christians trusting in their own feelings more than the word of God. (When they should be like Joshua in chapter 5-6, he was a man of war willing to "fight" but God said "march" around Jericho He didn't understand it but he trusted the word of the Lord anyway.) You may not understand your feelings but trust God's word anyway.

Don't ignore the Truth

Many don't understand the dangerous lifestyles they are living, they no longer want the truth or heed to the warnings signs the bible gives, they do not love truth, for they can not love God, Our Churches can not sorely preach, "The Love and Grace of God" and ignore the price of sin.

"The coming of the lawless one is according to the working of Satan, with all power, signs, and lying wonders, and with all unrighteous deception among those who perish, because they did not receive the love of truth, that they might be saved. And for this reason God will send them strong delusion, that they should believe the lie, that they all may be condemned who did not believe the truth but had pleasure in unrighteousness" 2 Thessalonians 2:9-12

"Know ye that the LORD he is God: it is he that hath made us, and not we ourselves; we are his people, and the sheep of his pasture." Psalms 100:3

"I Know also, my God, that thou tries the heart, and hast pleasure in uprightness." 1 Chronicles 29:17

You have read a lot of Scriptures and my Prayer, for you that you have a better understanding of the word God.

Lucifer was created as "an angel of light" but along the way he became something else, he became "the father of lies", John 8:44. So who do you think he is telling lie's to? The bible say's all lairs will end up in the pit.

"In sin did our mothers conceive us and we shapen iniquity Psalm 51:5, we have become easy prey to Satan and his devices, by not knowing and or reading the word of God for ourselves, only when we read and learn the word of God can we then keep God's commandments. Knowledge is indeed Power.

2 Tim 2:15/ Psalms 119:11

_____

_____

_____

All thoughts are created in our minds, if your mind is not stayed on him, what kind of thoughts will you have?

_____

_____

_____

Does John 8:44 holds the answer, what does it say?

_____

_____

_____

Whether consciously or subconsciously your life experiences shape you, but that's not it, and that's not all, being born again washing all that away you get a clear slate and learn to become a new person in Christ Jesus.

Write T for True or F for False in the space

1. If God doesn't answer your Prayers right away, then you should stop praying.

   _____

2. We should always be whatever we feel inside, no matter What? _____

3. The bible is for the people who lived 2000 years ago. _____

4. Does Obeying God's word show our love for him? _____

5. Is choosing "My will for my Life " wrong? _____

6. Can I still be close friends with My Old running Buddies? _____

7. "True" Christians are Homophobic? _____

8. It's up to me to help spread the gospel? _____

What does Romans 12 :1 mean? What is this scripture saying?

_____

_____

_____

_____

What does "Deny Himself" mean in Matt 16:24-25? How can you deny yourself?

_____

_____

_____

_____

Why is the "sin" mentioned in 1 Corinthians 6:17 a different type of sin, describe it in your own words?_

_____

_____

_____

Everyone will not want to hear what the Word of God has to say on this matter, what do you do then?

_____

_____

_____

According to Philippians 2:5 What kind of Mind Should we have?

_____

_____

_____

Why is it important?

_____

Taking Control

Prayer and Fasting along with reading your bible is Key to being delivered from any stronghold. Your fleshly desires can not rule over you if your ruling over it properly. The Prayer Clinic 2 by Clifton Jones, says, "men don't just fail the Lord because the devil is so strong, but because there is too weak." Mark 11:24 Your desire to live right has to be stronger than your desire was to commit sin.

What's Your Game Plan to be what God is calling for? What can you suggest to someone struggling in this area? Help Set some goals for them.

1. _____

_____

2. _____

_____

"Beloved, think it not strange concerning the fiery trail which is to try you, as though some strange thing happened unto you." 1 Peter 4:12

"And be not conformed to this world: but be ye transformed by the renewing of your mind, that ye may prove what is good, and acceptable, and perfect will of God," Romans 12:2

"Set your affection on things above, not on things on earth," Colossians 3:2

"Mortify therefore your members which are upon the earth; fornications, uncleanness, inordinate affection, evil concupiscence, which is idolatry." Colossians 3:5

You have to be willing to make lasting change in your life. You can't do it for anyone but yourself. Deciding to leave the life of Sexual Immorality or any sin, can be difficult.

What about the people you have built relationships with people, while living in sin, especially sexual sin. I found that the people I used to date and or hang with tried to hold me be back from truly living sin free, when I finally decided that I could no longer live in sin with them or anyone again. Once I told them I could not be apart of that lifestyle any longer they tired to hold me to my pass life. Always bringing it up, reminding me of the fun we used to have, Telling me to "Be Myself" and not let anyone or anything change me," Those people I ran with wouldn't take no for an answer they didn't want to just let me go. Or the spirit in them didn't. They started to lash out the more I said no, (kinda scary) I thought they would understand my decision, Maybe even still be my friends. Boy I was naïve.

"I wrote to you in my epistle not to keep company with sexually immoral people. Yet I certainly did not mean with the sexually immoral people of this world, or with covetous, or extortioners, or idolaters since then you would need to go out the world But now I have written to you not to keep company with any one named a brother who is sexually immoral or covetous, or an idolater, or a reviler, or a drunkard, or an extortioner not even to eat with such a person." 1 Corinthians 5:9-12

Needless to say It didn't work out, we couldn't be friends. I found out the hard way, these people I called my friends turned into enemies as soon as I couldn't be a party to sin any longer. Light can't fellowship with darkness, they can't coexist, 2 Corinthians 6:14

Those old friends can pull you back into sin if you let them, I had to cut ALL ties with my pass life, I even had to change my phone number. They had assumed that because I wanted to live a godly life that I was saying their life was not godly, in so many words. Words I had no said, but that's how these things go I had made a choice for me and I was sticking to it (this Time). All the old things had to go, people, cloths, I had to let it all go.

- Don't Cultivate old memories

- Recall the separation it caused you from God

- Remember your decision to walk with God

- Realize this new walk with God will take time

"… For I will forgive their iniquity, and I will remember their sin no more." Jeremiah 31:34

God remembers the sin but he doesn't charge it to you anymore, thank you Jesus

"Let this mind be in you, which was also in Christ Jesus:" Philippians 4:5

We have all sinned and fell short, that's no reason to keep living a sinful life. We must make a complete change! Renounce everything that is not like Christ, TODAY.

- "Wherein time past ye walked according to the course of this world, according to the prince of the power of the air, the spirit that now worketh in the children of disobedience: Among whom also we all had our conversation in times past in the lusts of our flesh, fulfilling the desires of the flesh and of the mind; and were by nature the children of wrath, even as others."

"Oh, what joy for those disobedience is forgiven, whose sins are put out of sight yes, what joy for those whose sin is no longer counted against them by the LORD." Romans 4: 7-8 NLT

Notes

Closing Section Prayer: Dear Lord, Thank you for this journey, I know you will enable me to take control of my life and provide all that I need to do it. Lord I have discovered through you that I can be what you are calling for me to be, remove the barriers and obstacles in my life so I can see you clearly, dear Lord Amen

STEP 3: WEEDING OUT PROCESS

Tensions can arise between nonbelieving "Friends" that you once hung with, they can hinder your walk with God if you let them. If they are not willing to change their ways, you will have to decide if you're going to discontinue spending time with them. Be aware they can pull you back into sin if you're not careful.

Understanding your flesh and it's desire will better equip you to make your stand for believing and doing the will of Christ. Abstain from sexual sins Leviticus 18:3-4, it's listed of what "not to do"

"Be holy because I, the Lord your God. Am holy." Leviticus 19:2

Mind	Body	Soul
Reminder of your pass life will and can hinder your walk, so get rid of them. Ephesians 5:8-11 Philippians 4:13	Spend time getting to know yourself, don't jump into dating right away. Deuteronomy 4:29	Spend time in the Word of God. (Holy Bible) James 4:7
Confess your sins, Declare "As an act of my will" I'm free From.. and name it Romans 4: 17	Pray & Fast, (deny your Body, Food and or water) This builds power in the spirit world in GOD. Mark 9:28	Anything that is not like Christ should be discontinued. Joshua 24:15
It is vital, to let old relationships go, that are not of God. 1 John 2:15- 17	Praise the Lord your God for what he has done for you. Psalm 42:11	Tell others of God's goodness, share your testimony. Revelation 11:12

"For what if some did not believe? Shall their unbelief make the faith of God without effect? God forbid: yea, let God be true, but every man a liar; as it is written, that thou mightest be justified in thy saying, and mightest overcome when thou art judged". Romans 3:3

When God was ready to give the Children of Israel the land of promise they were told not to make a covenant with them (don't live with them) Exodus 23 :32 -33 they had to be separate. Everything that is not like Christ must be rooted out.

In John L. Wallen paper titled, "Emotions as Problems, it state, "To interact with another is to risk having aroused in both of us. We can not turn on and turn off our feelings toward each other merely by hoping and wishing.

Jesus said to his disciples, "If any man will come after me, let him deny himself and take up his cross and follow me. For who so ever will save his life shall lose in and who so ever will lose his life for my sake shall find it." Matt 16: 24- 25

Homosexuality is Sin and like all sexual Immorality it's sin against God. Sin is Terminal without change. The Lord gave them up to uncleanness because of the lust of our hearts, Satan took something so basic, as being a man or a woman and add doubt, to the point that we that we as a people don't know, who, (man or Woman) who's (God's Child) or what (his master piece) we are.

"God's faithfulness is proved not by the elimination of hardships but by carrying us through them. Change is not the absence of struggles; change is the freedom to choose holiness in the midst of our struggles. I realized that the ultimate issue has to be that I yearn after God in total surrender and complete obedience." Christopher Yuan

"I struggle with same-sex attraction, but when I struggle I look to the cross and see Jesus hanging there it makes me want to fight. If Jesus sacrificed his life for me to go to heaven, then I can sacrifice this sinful lifestyle for him." Unknown

"Knowing this, that our old man is crucified with him, that the body of sin might be destroyed, that henceforth we should not serve sin." Romans 6:6

The DNA is in!

If looking between your legs is not enough, than your DNA and chromosomes hold the answer. Men and Women have at Minimum of 6,500 genetic differences between them, every cell is affected by your DNA. If you really sit back and think about it you will see that two men's bodies just were not meant to be together sexually neither were two women's bodies it just doesn't fit together, no matter how you try.

It was not in God's design for a penis to enter into a rectum. A rectum was designed for elimination purposes. Continued penetrating of the rectal area will cause the anal walls to become weak, making them unable to hold waste, and over time incontinent altogether. Homosexuality is an unnatural, misuse of your body.

Homosexuality is contrary to God's design for sexuality. Therefore homosexuality is a sin and we must stand firm to God's truths, Sex and sexuality was God's design and therefore he and he alone holds the blueprints of the design of it's purpose. "Remember that all sin is a disruption of God's design." Fritz Chery

Numerous Studies have been done, and the Attempted Suicide Rate is 1.5 to 3 times higher for LGBTQ youth than Heterosexual youth. Young people are struggling to cope and we need to help them fast and in a hurry, and not by making them feel like lepers. They need to know that there is help for them if the wish it. There is a better way in Christ, he has created a way of escape for those who will seek it.

You really don't want to be turned over to your our lusts:

Pray this Prayer,

Father God, forgive me of all my sins, seen and unseen, I don't want to remain a sinner, Lord find grace in my sight, help me, teach me your ways that I might not sin against you further. I offer to you from this day to the next my life as a living sacrifice, Renew my mind create in me a clean heart that I may follow you all the days of my life Amen.

When you focus your mind is on Christ Jesus, those other thoughts can't enter into your mind. When, not "if" a sinful thought enters into your my read your bible.. and watch that thought go. It sounds to good to be true, but it works. Can't take a paper bible with you ever where download the bible app

We are in a War Saints of God… and you MUST have your Weapons Ready

- A Bible in hand
- Know At least 1 Scripture by heart (Try out, Isaiah 55:6-7)
- Blessed oil
- A person you can call on for a Quick Prayer or encouragement

How can you as a Christian help "John" live better Christian life?

_____

_____

_____

When your old friends start calling you after you have given yourself back to the LORD How can you tell your old running buddy's your not going to hang out with them any more?

_____

_____

_____

How does cleaning out your mental closet help you physically ?

_____

_____

_____

Now that you are on the road to being a called out believer, it is a good idea to find a job in your church? True or False

How long should you wait before dating? Don't allow yourself to be placed in any sexual situations. Be careful / prayerful to not Replace one sin for another.

Joining the Men's or Women's ministry can help you in your Christian walk?

True or False

Why?

_____

_____

Closing Section Prayer: Dear Lord, I thank you for all that you are doing in my life, You have opened my mind to a better way to serve you and your people, thank you for the opportunity to experience you fully, give me the strength to trust your instructions for me more perfectly Lord I praise you for the freedom I now have in you Amen.

SECTION 3: PEDOPHILIA

Pedophiles can be found in all walks of life, and social class, and races both male and female. They for the most part very discrete due to their sexual interest in children, and the fear of being found out. There are vast differences in what is defended as a "Pedophile". I've found the majority are men who are interested in boys, most have a specific preferences in age, but not all. There are women also who are "attracted" children. It's important to say not all pedophiles act out their desires.

Pedophilia goes by other names, M.A.P. "Minor Attracted Persons," Man -Boy, Love." To break it down, it's an adult who is attracted to a child, and wants to have a sexual relationship with them. They use words like "Attracted To" or "Love", care for that is just some of what I found in my internet search. Pedophilia is a sin, it is sexual immorality.

There are more and more people opening up about "being a Pedophile" on the internet in an afford to make everyone understand what they are about. My internet search found a few stories of people willing to share their "pro views" on the subject which is understandable because of the these people are viewed. Needless to say there are very strong views on the subject.

Groups have started a movement to normalize pedophilia, many are trying to come in on the LGBTQ wave of "gay marriage" being made legal and believe it or not some law makers are listening. Even though the outcry is greatly in favor of our children.

People have these "feelings" and we're going to talk about it. Having sexual relationships with children can cause great harm to a child 's mind and body. this is a fact, that many of us share. Children are not toys to be played with. We as a people have allowed these doors to be opened, sexual immorality has not crept in, it's flooded in. you can't as a people accept certain sins and push others out, we must say no to all sin. We have become accepting to homosexuality by feeling like "let the do what they want to do" "it doesn't affect me" but it does Satan won't stop there.

There is a concept going around the internet that children should be able to have sex with an adult if they wish to, that they should be able to give consent. It's said that, "pedophilia" is a "sexual orientation" and it's being compared to "being born gay or straight." What has our society opened itself up to? Pedophiles are following the lead of the LGBTQ community. This is insane.

"Even so it is not the will of your father which is in heaven, that one of these little ones should perish." Matthew 18:14

If the Lord doesn't want them lost or to perish then, does the Lord want them sexually used for their bodies? The answer is NO! that is sin we must not partake in sin and help those who are struggling with sins if they want to be helped. God is able to help you overcome any and all sin, if you ask him.

Address Sin, Stop it in it's tracks, be honest with yourself.

"Take heed that ye despise not one of these little ones; for I say unto you, that in heaven their angles do always behold the face of my father which is in heaven. For the Son of man is come to save that which was lost." Matthew 18: 10-11

Can God save a pedophile? I believe God can and will, if called upon. Sexual Immorality, is sin, in the fact that it displeases God, there is a need to call on the Lord for renewing of the mind, the very act of having sex with a child can be very harmful to the child and have a lasting affect. It would take away our children's innocence one of the very things that makes them a child. It would stand to reason that if you profess to "love a child" you would wish them No harm, at all period, when you think about it this act is a very selfish act to say the least, LOVE is not involved in no way, shape or form what so ever in my opinion.

"And Jesus called a little child unto him, and set him in the midst of them, And said, Verily I say unto you, Except ye be converted, and become as little children, ye shall not enter into the kingdom of heaven." Matthew 18:2-6

A child's faith can surpass a man's faith, because of their innocent, and willingness to believe. A child can believe where a man, sometimes won't allow himself to believe. "Whosoever therefore shall humble himself as this little child, the same is greatest in the kingdom of heave." The attributes of a child meekness, humbleness his/her loving nature would all be destroyed if men where to impose their will on children. If allowed, these acts, man as a whole would be so far gone. I believe spirits play a big part in this lifestyle. Whatever sin they influence man to commit, or try to make "normal" we as Christians need to be on the look out for. They desire to distort all God has put into place. Instead of doing God's will, our creator man has decided to please himself. By getting man to sin repeatedly on a national scale the devil is sending a message, that these people you created have turned away from God and are following their own desires which will land them in hell.

"But whoso shall offend one of these little ones which believe in me, it were better for him a millstone were hanged about his neck, and that he were drowned in the depth of the sea." Matthew 18:6

"It were better for him that a millstone were hanged about his neck, and he cast into the sea, than that he should offend one of these little ones." Luke 17:2

"Flee fornication. Every sin that a man doeth is without the body; but he that committeth fornication sinneth against his own body." 1 Corinthians 6:18

"But fornication, and all uncleanness, or covetousness, let it not be once named among you, as becometh saints; Neither filthiness, nor foolish talking, nor jesting, which are not convenient: but rather giving of thanks. For this ye know, that no whoremonger, nor unclean person, nor covetous man, who is an idolater, hath any inheritance in the kingdom of Christ and of God." Ephesians 5:3-5

"Submit yourselves therefore to God. Resist the devil, and he will flee from you." James 4:7

God can deliver you from any and all sexual immoralities if you let him. Research for yourself and see what's really going on in our world today. Who are your actions serving? Many times our actions are a far cry from who we say we are.

John tells you he was molested as a kid by his dad's male friend a few times and he thinks that's why he is gay? What would you say to him?

_____

_____

_____

_____

Closing Section Prayer: Dear Lord, I know there is nothing to hard for you, guide me in all your ways so I can be a testimony of your saving grace, Lord I want to be what you are calling for in these last days Amen.

SECTION 4: HERE COMES THE COPY CAT

If you have a younger Brother or Sister, (like I do) then you know how much a copy cat can annoy you. Satan is the biggest Copy Cat.

GOD Author, Creator	Satan Copy Cat
1. Marriage Man + Woman	1. Same sex Marriage
2. "God's will be done" Matt 6:9-13	2. "Do what thy Wilt" What you Want
3. The Holy Cross	3. Upside down Cross
4. The Rainbow Genesis 9	4. LGBTQ Rainbow flag
5. 7 colors in the Rainbow (7 meaning Completion)	5. 6 colors of rainbow flag (6 mark of the beast)
6. The 10 Commandment Exodus 20	6. The Law of Thelema (11 Principles of Thelemites Self proclaim worshipers Satan / Self= I

Coincidence, I think not.
Feel free to use your Google search engine to look up these facts.

Pagan worship included idol worship and in most cases it involved sexual acts, and murder of Children as in Elijah's day in 1 Kings 18. King Ahab and his wife Jezebel worshiped Baal They chose to worship other gods instead of The God of Israel following those gods, preforming ritual child sacrifices and acts of Prostitution

Satan tempted Jesus

Jesus was lead of the spirit to the wilderness to be tempted of the devil, Jesus had fasted for 40 days and was hungry, Satan the tempter said to him "If" thou be the Son of God command that these stones be made bread (Satan already knew who Jesus was that's why he was there) yet and still he used the word if, as if to say "prove it". But Jesus came to him with the word of God, "Man shall not live by bread alone, but by every word that proceedeth out of the mouth of God". Each time the devil tempted Jesus, Jesus came back with the word of God, Satan tried to tempt Jesus 3 times in the book of Matthew 4:1- 11, Jesus is our great example of how we can stand and win against the devil.

"Be sober, be vigilant; because your adversary the devil, as a roaring lion, walketh about, seeking whom he may devour". 1 Peter 5:8 "As a roaring lion", A Copy Cat, (get it cat/ lion) okay I'll keep my day job. This scripture tells us to be sober and watchful, Satan is looking to get any and everyone he can to sin. The next verse # 9 "Whom resist steadfast in faith, knowing that the same afflictions are accomplished in your brethren that are in the world." You can resist you do not have to give into your flesh.

"For we ourselves also were sometimes foolish, disobedient, deceived, serving divers lusts and pleasures, living in malice and envy, hateful, and hating one another. But after that the kindness and love of God our Savior toward man appeared, Not by works of righteousness which we have done, but according to his mercy he saved us, by the washing of regeneration, and renewing of the Holy Ghost;" Titus 3:3-5

You need the Holy Ghost to fight the devil and any lustful desires you can't do it on your own. Obey Acts 2:38-39, "Then Peter said unto them, Repent, and bee baptized everyone of you in the name of Jesus Christ for the remission of sin, and ye shall receive the gifts of the Holy Ghost . For the promise is unto you, and to your children, and to all that are afar off, even as many as the Lord our God shall."

"There hath no temptation taken you but such as is common to man: but God is faithful, who will not suffer you to be tempted above that ye are able; but will with the temptation also make a way to escape, that ye may be able to bear it." 1 Corinthians 10:13

God is so awesome that, he even made a way of escape for us, he will not tempt us more than we can handle .. that means you are able to stand and over come the temptation that comes your way. Now that's a reason to SHOUT for joy

"Submit yourselves therefore to God. Resist the devil, and he will flee from you." James 4:7

Surrender your desire, and give God control

Sin Has Consequences

"If I sin and in the process of sinning break my arm, when I find forgiveness from sin, I still have to deal with a broken bonne." Chuck Swindoll

Sin causes us separation from God, the bible informs us of the different consequences sin can cause, like loss of life, reprobated mind, sorrows, hopelessness, depression, suicide, pain, sickness and so on some of these results can only be removed by supernatural means. Some consequences can change if you change your ways (stop sinning, and repent)

Lets look at two examples:

The woman at the well, in John 8, she was found in sin, the law required her life by stoning her, but Jesus offered her forgiveness of sin.

Judas Iscariot Luke 22, number with the twelve, the betrayer of Jesus conspired for money sought opportunity to betray him, When Jesus was on the cross he said Forgive them for they no not what they do. But Judas of Iscariot no doubt struggling with depression and sadness couldn't bear the thought and hung himself, sin caused separation from God which lead ultimately to his death.

Reconciliation to God is possible after one has sinned, with true heart felt repentance. Admit that we were wrong and have sinned against God offer him our life and live for him, and do his will.

The Holy Ghost will speak to your heart to help you beat each temptation from sin. It is very important to know your bible, it is a weapon your tool to Stand tall when temptations come. Use it's examples to aid you.

How did Satan Deceive Eve, in the garden in the book of Genesis?

_____

_____

_____

What should Eve have done differently?

_____

_____

_____

What insight did you get when you read, My Story in my book, "Adam and Steve, My Flesh, My Desire"?

_____

_____

_____

How do you relate to my Story, in my previous book?

_____

_____

_____

"John" doesn't think the devil has anything to gain by him being gay or even him living a gay lifestyle. What would you now tell John?

_____

_____

_____

What scriptures from Adam and Steve, My Flesh, My Desire helped you the most?

_____

_____

_____

In Chapter 7 of My Book Adam and Steve, My Flesh, My Desire.. What did you think about the parents, and how they handled their children's behavior?

_____

_____

_____

If a child can't choose to have cake for dinner, or to stay up till 1:00 am on a school night, what makes you think that a child is able to choose what gender they want to be?

_____

_____

_____

Did you think the parents played a part in their child's lifestyle?

_____

When does supporting your child go too far?

_____

_____

_____

Which group of parents stood out more to you on page 41- 44 of Adam and Steve, My Flesh, My Desire? And Why?

_____

_____

_____

Have you seen parents who don't clearly define gender lines in their homes?

_____

_____

_____

Is teaching a child the clear differences between boys and girls old fashioned?

_____

_____

_____

What is Proverbs chapter 19:26-27 saying?

_____

_____

In Revelations 12:11, How did they overcome? By what_____and the
_____ of their _____.

In the Book of Exodus chapter 7, we see first hand that Satan is a "Copy Cat" he can not "create" only distort truth, remember he was created to, by God. Satan cannot have an original thought.

Exodus 7:10-12 "Moses and Aaron went unto Pharaoh, and did so as the Lord had commanded: and Aaron cast down his rod before Pharaoh, and before his servants, and it became a serpent. Then Pharaoh also called the wise men and the sorcerers: now the magicians of Egypt, they also did in like manner with their enchantment. For they cast down every man his rod, and they became serpents: but Aaron's rod swallowed up their rod."

Who won that battle?

_____

The bible describes in detail, who and what Satan is, what his nature is like, his actions, his character and where he will end up! Satan is like a fisher man, he baits his hook according to the appetite of the fish he is searching for.

To be able to beat him you must know what to look out for.

"He that committeth sin is of the devil; for the devil sinneth from the beginning. For this purpose the son of God was manifested, that he might destroy the works of the devil." 1 John 3:8

"Ye are of your father the devil, and the lusts of your father ye will do. He was a murderer from the beginning, and abode not in the truth, because there is no truth in him. When he speaketh of his own: for he is a liar, and the father of it." John 8:44

Have you gotten a clear picture of Satan yet?

Or What he wants from you?

Why was the Son of God Manifested?

_____

_____

If you are doing these things you are not a child of Christ.

Read each of these Scriptures for More Light

"And if it seem evil unto you to serve the LORD, choose you this day whom ye will serve; whether the gods which your father served that were on the other side of the flood, or the gods of the Amorites, in whose land ye dwell: but as for me and my house, we will serve the LORD." Joshua 24: 15

How will you use your free will? Who will you serve?

_____

_____

"Jesus answered them, Verily, verily, I say unto you, whosoever committeth sin is the servant of sin." John 8:34

"Seek ye the LORD while he may be found, call ye upon him while he is near: Let the wicked forsake his way, and the unrighteous man his thoughts: and let him return unto the LORD, and he will have mercy upon him; and to our God, for he will abundantly pardon." Isaiah 55: 6-7

What is this scripture telling you?

_____

_____

_____

"For I am jealous over you with godly jealousy: for I have espoused you to one husband that I may present you as a chaste virgin to Christ. But I fear, lest by any means, as the serpent beguiled Eve through his subtlety, so your minds should be corrupted from the simplicity that is in Christ." 2 Corinthians 11: 2-3 that verse right there..!

God doesn't want to share you, he wants you, he wants you all to himself, he doesn't even want you in a position to be tricked. There is so much meat here in this verse. Break this scripture down. What stands out here to you?

_____

_____

_____

And if it can be picked up, it can be put down!
If it can be learned, it can be unlearned!

God is calling for you to be a new creature 2 Cor 5:17
"Therefore if any man be in Christ, he is a new creature: old things are passed away; behold all thing are become new."

God is call for a New Creature, Your old man, Your old desires, no matter what it is needs to be put to death.

You don't have to be that person anymore, from this day forward repent from Sin Right now Today!

Turn Away completely

John 3:16 " For God so loved the world, that he gave his only begotten Son, that whosoever believeth in him should not perish, but have everlasting life."

What did Jesus himself say about marriage being between a man and a woman?

_____

_____

_____

Matthew 19:4, And he answered and said unto them, "Have ye not read, that he which made them at the beginning made them male and female,"

Man and Woman were designed by God, it was so since the beginning of time.
Which Scripture/ Scripture's helped you the most? Which scripture would you recommend to someone who is struggling in these areas?

_____

_____

_____

Why?

_____

_____

_____

Why is it important not be involved in Sexual immorality, or any sin?

_____

_____

_____

Closing section Prayer: Dear Lord, Everyday you provide me, is a blessing and an opportunity to grow more in you, Lord I'm leaning on you and getting stronger, I am committed to your ways, continue to clean out any and everything unlike you, you are my rock, my help in troubles. Amen

SECTION 5: UNDERSTANDING SPIRITS

The term "Evil Spirits," goes hand in hand with "Demons and Devils" in the passages of scripture. As you read each one of these scriptures you will see the influence of spirits had on the people who they inhabited.

Read and Compare

"And it came to pass afterward, that he went throughout every city and village, preaching and showing the glad tiding of the kingdom of God: and the 12 were with him, And certain women, which had been healed of evil spirits and infirmities, Mary called Magdalene, out of whom went 7 devils," Luke 8:1

"And when he went forth to land, there met him out of the city a certain man, which had devils long time, and wore no cloths, neither abode in any house, but in tombs. When he saw Jesus, he cried out, and fell down before him, and with a loud voice said, What have I to do with thee, Jesus, thou Son of God most high? I beseech thee, torment me not. (For he had commanded the unclean spirit to come out of the man. For oftentimes it had caught him: and he was kept bound with chains and in fetters; and be broke the bands, and was driven of the devil into the wilderness.) And asked him, saying What is thy name? And he said, Legion: because many devils were entered into him. And they besought him that he would not command them to go out into the deep. And there was there an herd of many swine feeding on the mountain: and they besought him that he would suffer them to enter into them. And he suffered them. Then went the devils out of the man, and entered into swine: and the herd ran violently down a steep place into the lake, and were choked. When they that fed them saw what was done, they fled, and went and told it in the city and in the country. Then they went out to see what was done; and came to Jesus, and found the man, out of whom the devils were departed, sitting at the feet of Jesus, clothed, and in his right mind: and they were afraid. They also which saw it told them by what means he that was possessed of the devils was healed," Luke 8:27-36

Notice the behavior of the man/ Legion before and after he met Jesus.. What were some of the differences you noticed? How did he act before he met Jesus?

_____

_____

_____

Compare the four Gospel accounts of "Legion", what stands out to you as you learn more about him?

How did this man act /carry himself after he was healed/ delivered?

_____

_____

_____

Just My Thoughts

I don't have scripture for this, but I have a thought, because he was a man his personality was established already, you could see the change in him as noted...

But in a child when a spirit enters them wouldn't it be a bit harder to tell, might we as adults write it off as a child acting out? Could this be part of the reason spirits inhabit children more and more?

Here the swine/ pigs seem to have decided that they didn't want spirits living in them. Mark gives an account of this man's live also in more detail Mark 5: 2-20. Read the account of this man in all four gospels.

"And when they were come to the multitude, there came to him a certain man, kneeling down to him, and saying, Lord have mercy on my son: for he is a lunatic, and sore vexed: for ort times he falleth into the fire, and oft into the water. And I bought him to thy disciples, and they could not cure him. Then Jesus said, o faithless and perverse generation, how long shall I be with you? How long shall I suffer you? Bring him hither to me and Jesus rebuked the devil; and he departed out of him: and the child was cured from that very hour. Then came the disciples to Jesus apart, and said, why could not we cast him out? And Jesus said unto them, because of your unbelief: for verily I say unto you, If ye have faith as a grain of mustard seed ye shall say unto this mountain, remove hence to yonder place; and it shall remove; and nothing shall be impossible unto you. Howbeit this kind goeth not out but by Prayer and Fasting." Matthew 17: 14-21

_____

_____

_____

This scripture confirms that all spirits are not equal, some are stronger and require Prayer and Fasting to deliver a the person being used by a evil spirit.

Acts 16: 16-18 Read about the girl who could tell the future by a spirit. Notice how she behaved.

_____

_____

_____

_____

Luke tells us Satan entered Judas Iscariot,

Did being a theft leave him open for Satan to enter him? Yes or No.. and Why?

_____

_____

_____

How can we keep Satan from entering us?

_____

_____

_____

"John" feels like he is just being himself, when he desires same sex companions,

What Scriptures can you now show him to open his eyes to the truth?

_____

_____

_____

Closing Section Prayer: Dear Lord, Bless your mighty name I realize when I take it one day at a time, I'm able to depend on you more perfectly, help me not to rush the process. My success depends solely on you, Lord I realized I can't do this on my own, you have blessed me thus far and I will continue rely on you, everyday Lord keep my mind stayed on you, as I move forward in Jesus name I pray Amen.

What's your prayer for "John" deliverance?

_____

_____

_____

SECTION 6: PRAYER & FASTING: THE MEAT & POTATOES

Why is Prayer & Fasting so important?

Prayer and Fasting is a way for you to get closer to God, and for you to hear from him. Prayer and fasting paves the way to having the mind of Christ. It is a weapon unlike any other as we have read in the last Section, it will help you to battle the enemy and everyday struggles. Prayer and Fasting teaches you how to walk the Christian walk. It shows God we are serious and totally dependent on him alone.

Fasting Tips

Fast on a day that is Not Hectic for You

Use a Prayer Wheel, add what you're praying
for GOD to do.

Use your hunger pains as prompts to pray
more.

EXPECT Spiritual Opposition "Satan"
Doesn't want you to get your break through,
he will try to interrupt your fasting time.

Drink water to combat dizziness if you need to.

We are to always pray, (talking to the Lord). Fasting and Praying, denying your body food and or water, sex (if married 1 Corinthians 7:5) for a time.

Prayer & Fasting is not to be seen of man for you to boast of how godly you are, but instead a time to be in the presences of the Lord (humbly asking, crying out, a total surrender of self to him)

There are many benefits to Prayer and Fasting, the intimacy with God is amazing. Prayer and Fasting involves discipline, to push your plate back and not eat, to deny your flesh food or any thing else it may want. Don't let feeling of I can't do this stop you. Pick a day wake up and tell God thank you, before your feet touch the carpet leave the T.V off no checking your cell Talk to God, spend the day with him in prayer, read his word (the bible) listen you up lifting gospel music all day.

"Blessed are they which do hunger and thirst after righteousness: for they shall be filled," Matthew 5:6

As with any Fast if you are on Any Medication ask your Doctor First

"If my people, which are called by my name, shall humble themselves, and pray, and seek my face, and turn from their wicked ways; then will I hear from heaven, and forgive their sin, and will heal their land." 2 Chronicles 7:14

Living in sin keeps us separate from God, that's not God's will for you. By seeking the Lord with our Mind, Body and Soul can we have the weapons we need to with stand the wilds of the devil, Satan that serpent that old dragon?

"Finally, my brethren, be strong in the LORD and in the power of his might. Put on the whole armor of God that you may be able to stand against the wiles of the devil. For we do not wrestle against flesh and blood, but against spiritual wickedness in high place. Wherefore take unto you the whole armor of God that ye may be able to withstand in the evil day, and having done all to stand. Stand therefore, having your loins girt about in truth, and having on the breastplate of righteousness; And your feet shod with the preparation of the gospel of peace; Above all, taking the shield of faith, wherewith ye shall be able to quench all the fiery darts of the wicked one. And take the helmet of salvation and the sword of the Spirit, which is the word of God: Praying always with all supplication in the Spirit, and watching thereunto with all perseverance and supplication for all saints." Ephesians 6:10-18

The writer Paul tells us we are in a spiritual war and he gives us the tools we need to win. Satan's power is limited that's why he uses tricks, schemes, he is crafty and will mislead you, he will use the weakness of a man's flesh and prey on it, these fiery darts are temptations he sends our way in hopes that you will fall for them, and do them.

What does the New Testament scriptures have to say, about Sexual Immorality?

Romans 1:24-32, "Wherefore God also gave them up to uncleanness through the lusts of their own hearts, to dishonor their own bodies between themselves: Who changed the truth of God into a lie, and worshiped and served the creature more than the creator, who is blessed forever. Amen

For this cause God gave them up unto vile affections: for even their women did change the natural use into that which is against nature:

And likewise also the men, leaving the natural use of the woman, burned in their lust one toward another; men with men working that which is unseemly, and receiving in themselves that recompense of their error which was meet.

And even as they did not like to retain God in their knowledge, God gave them over to a reprobate mind, to do those things which are not convenient;

Being filled with all unrighteousness, fornication, wickedness, covetousness, maliciousness; full of murder, debate, deceit, malignity; whisperers, Backbiters, haters of God, despiteful, proud, boasters, inventors of evil things, disobedient to parents 31.) Without understanding, covenant breakers, without natural affection, implacable, unmerciful: Who knowing the judgment of God, that they which commit such things are worthy of death, not only do the same, but have pleasure in them that do them."

Here Paul has a strong opinion on sexual immorality and goes further to say it is unnatural sex, and it is to be enjoyed between a husband and a wife. But lust of the flesh has corrupted this gift

The bible is our guide and we must follow it, anything else is ungodly and of the world.

Test your Knowledge

What does the bible say about Sexual immorality, Homosexuality and Bestiality?

_____

_____

_____

_____

_____

Do the Old Testament Scriptures support the New Testament Scriptures? Why?

_____

_____

_____

_____

What did God tell Moses to tell the Children of Israel NOT to do in their promised land? Where is it found?

_____

_____

_____

_____

_____

_____

Why is Prayer and Fasting so important according to the book of Matthew?

_____

_____

_____

Draw a line and Match the Scripture with the Verse, by looking them up:

James 5:13   Is not this the fast that I have chosen? To lose the bands
              Of wickedness, to undo the heavy burdens, and to let the
              Oppressed go free, and that ye break every yoke?

Psalms 35: 13   Is any among you afflicted? Let him pray. Is any merry?
                 Let him sing psalms.

Isaiah 58:6   But as for me, when they were sick, my clothing was sack-
               Cloth: I humbled my soul with fasting; and my prayer
               Returned into mine own bosom.

There is a thin line between Love and Acceptance

"Unconditional love does not equal unconditional approval of my behavior." Christopher Yuan-

We have to be sure what kinds of messages we send to others, when it comes to loving them vs. accepting their lifestyles.

Just because you love someone doesn't mean you have to accept their choices, behavior or lifestyle, We must tell them in LOVE what the BIBLE says, it's our job as a Christian, to let them know that they are living a sinful life, Don't just single out Homosexuals (They just happen to be who God has directed me to enlighten) let them know they can change if they want to. If someone wants to change, their lifestyle, we, as Christians can show them how they can do it through the Word of GOD and brotherly Love.

"Give thanks unto the Lord, call upon his name, and make known his deeds among the people. Sing unto him, sing psalms unto him, talk ye of all his wondrous works. Glory ye in his holy name: let the heart of them rejoice that seek the LORD. Seek the LORD and his strength, seek his face continually. Remember his marvelous works that he hath done, his wonders, and the judgments of his mouth."1 Chronicles 16: 8 – 12

Congratulations!!!

Now that we're at the end of the Workbook, let's go back and look at the goals you set for your life.

Have you met your goals?

Do you plan on continuing reading the scriptures that were laid out?

How do you feel now?

Do you feel like you have a greater knowledge of the unseen world around you?

Have you cleaned out your Mental Closet? As time passes have you noticed that it gets easier and easier?

What things do you still need to Work on?

How do you plan on addressing these issues?

The good thing about this workbook is that the principles apply to every type of Sexual Sin. I've noticed that when I didn't met my goals the way I have planned to, I dropped the ball somewhere, don't give up, retrace your steps, Reread this book if necessary to address each issue your facing and apply the ideas and principles within, if you have any questions email me @: Drww009@yahoo.com.

Make time to Pray today.

REFERENCES

The King James Holy Bible .... KJV

The Living Bible .... Tyndale House Foundation 1971

Bible readers Companion .... By Lawrence O. Richards

Prayer Clinic 2 .... By Clifton Jones

Emotions as Problems .... By John L. Wallen

Adam & Steve: My Flesh, My Desire .... By Minister Debbie Williams

The Apostolic Way .... The Pentecostal Assemblies of the World. INC.,

Christian Counseling ....Gary R. Collins, Ph.D.

A few Books I Recommend You to Reading

The New Birth.. Leroy Chappelle

The Old Man is Dead.. Edgar A. Posey, D.D, Ph.D.

Adam and Steve My flesh, my desire... Min Debbie Williams

Lord Heal Me from the Inside.. Clifton Jones

ABOUT THE AUTHOR

Dr. Debbie Williams and her, husband La'Mond Williams now live in Lake Charles Louisiana, with their children. She has also written "Riddle Me This" A Christian riddle book, full of riddles derived from the King James Version of the bible, these riddles range from easy to hard, and can give you a better understanding of the bible. "Adam and Steve: My Flesh, My Desire" A book that gives insight not only about Homosexuality, but how God delivered her from it. Her desire is to help someone along the way to be free from "Strongholds" of a Sexual Immoral lifestyle. She has a love for the children of GOD.

She received her Ministry License in March 8, 2002, from the Pentecostal Assemblies of the World (P.A.W.). She also earned, a Bachelor of Arts in Biblical Studies in 2016. She also earned a Doctorate of Theology in Christian Ministry and a Doctorate in Christian Counseling with an emphasis in Sexual Identity Issues from California University of Theology in 2018.

She is a faithful member Of, Word of Life Outreach Ministries, in Palmdale California where her Pastor is Suff. Bishop Jeryld D. Ross, 1st Lady Alice Ross. She currently is working as the Women's Ministry president, Intermittent Sunday School teacher and Altar Worker and assist's willingly wherever needed.

Debbie also has a passion for Crafts, Painting, Journal Making, She likes to say she has a "crafting spirit" straight from God, because he is a crafter, after all he created the heavens and the earth. Genesis 1:1

She drove twelve years for Metropolitan Transportation Authority (M.T.A) in the City of Los Angeles California, where she met the love of her life.

"Have ye not read, that he which made them at the beginning made them male and female," Matthew 19:4

Printed in the United States
by Baker & Taylor Publisher Services